WAKING
THE DEAF DOG

WAKING
THE DEAF DOG

POEMS BY

MICHAEL DAVID MADONICK

Avocet Press Inc   New York

Published by
Avocet Press Inc
19 Paul Court
Pearl River, NY 10965
http://www.avocetpress.com
books@avocetpress.com

AVOCET PRESS

Cover Design: Richard Powers
Cover Art:
   TAMAYO, Rufino.
   Detail of <u>Animals</u>. 1941.
   Oil on Canvas, 30 1/8 x 40" (76.5 x 101.6 cm).
   The Museum of Modern Art, New York. Inter-American Fund.
   Photograph ©1999 The Museum of Modern Art, New York.

Library of Congress Cataloging-in-Publication Data

Madonick, Michael David
      Waking the deaf dog : poems by Michael David Madonick. --1st ed.
            p.   cm.
      ISBN 0-9661072-8-4
      I. Title
PS3563.A3424W3   1999
811´ .54— dc21
                                                            99-39891
                                                            CIP

Printed in the USA
First Edition

for Brigit, Chris, Maria, Macklin and Anna
1 / 4 / 7

ACKNOWLEDGMENTS

American Literary Review: "Bull"

Ascent: "The Practice Field" and "Upon Discovering The Means By Which The Waters May Flow"

Boulevard: "Revelation In The Lobby Of The Grand Hotel"

Chicago Review: "Imperatives, for Robert Ardrey"

Cimarron Review: "The Pirate Map" and "On Moving To Illinois"

Controlled Burn: "Rumor"

Crab Orchard Review: "The Inconvenience Of The Spirit"

Creeping Bent: "White Deer"

New England Review: "The Sardine Can" and "Settled In"

New Jersey Poetry Journal: "Letter To My Ex-Wife Who Is Having Lunch With Harold Bloom Tomorrow"

Pembroke: "That Wing"

River Styx: "Innocence"

Spoon River Poetry Review: "The Promise"

Southern Humanities Review: "The Professor"

Sycamore Review: "Abide," "Gravity," and "Peas"

Tamaqua: "Declination," "Hiding," and "Tourists In The Wrong Climate"

Tar River Poetry: "The Umlaut" and "Waking The Deaf Dog"

Waikato Journal: "Today"

LITERATURE, A Contemporary Introduction; James Hurt, ed. 1994. Macmillan College Publishing Company, New York. "Letter To My Ex-Wife Who Is Having Lunch with Harold Bloom Tomorrow" and "White Deer"

TABLE OF CONTENTS

PART 1

PART 2

PART 3

Men, unlike mockingbirds, have the capacity for systematic self-delusion. We echo each other with equal precision, equal eloquence, equal assurance. But be it said for mockingbirds, hidden by the indigo of a California night, that they do not risk their species' future with the lush inflation of their song.

Robert Ardrey, *The Territorial Imperative*

PART I

WAKING THE DEAF DOG

It used to be the light would wake him, just
the stirring of things, the joints of sparrows

stretching their wings, one at a time in the oak.
Now, he sleeps against the vibration of the Frigidaire

until I come down from writing upstairs, or my
son does, and we stomp our feet next to his head

like we're killing ants. When he finally wakes,
he isn't happy or sad, he's stunned, confused,

the way a newborn hangs bat-like from the doctor's
hand waiting for a start, anything that means go.

Were it not for my wife's intervention he'd be soap
now, after he bit my son, a year ago, above his right

eye, where a scar, just a shade whiter than his skin,
holds like a grain of rice to his forehead. I don't hate

this dog. After all I traded my good parrot, Toby,
for him, the Grey-Cheek that dive-bombed the kids

under tables and chairs. I just wish he'd listen, turn
to me the way Toby did and repeat something I say.

At times, I envy, I suppose, the deepness of his sleep,
where rabbits run across heavy lawns and song birds

and crows are merely playing parts in some yellowed
silent film. When he's outside, using his nose up and

down the driveway, snaring the scents of Spring or
the neighbor's bitch beginning heat, I wonder if he

pushes his dead ears for a signal, wants, if he could
to cup one with a paw. My dog is deaf but I yell at him

anyway, when he begins to wander down toward
the street. Or, when he sits in the sun like a lawn-jockey

reading the wind. I could be kinder, but how? How
does one move a deaf dog who bites?

THE SARDINE CAN

This is what the world needs! A key.

And as I turn the tin sarcophagus back,
they lie there front to back, back

to front like batteries, alternating poles or
lovers charged in some final

indecent act. Keats would imagine them
as mummies clutching the broken promise

to their chests among the fine
apothecary store of organs. What is good

is that they are foreign. Portuguese,
I think. So they can be trusted. Even better,

they are headless, their joy complete. Without
tails there is no maneuvering, no

ferry of slaves to row them across
the river. Yet, I am here, like John

Donne with a plastic fork, lifting their gauze
of elegant bone, such flimsy ladders, on which

the metaphysica of their souls, the promenade
of odor, climbs into this, my dirty kitchen,

their blinking florescent end.

POINT OF ENTRY

The wind is telling the trees what to do. Even the grass
picks up the message. There are times I'll stand by

the empty clothesline and listen to the odd vibration it makes,
taut as it is, between the oaks. I'll touch it, the way

one touches water in the early morning, a lake, where
water-spiders look like a thousand busy hands pushing up and

down for a door, any point of entry. I don't know what I want
to hear. If, in fact, there's anything to be told. But

I often stand out in the breeze, medial,
expecting anything, even luck.

SETTLED IN

My new neighbors keep asking, are you
settled in? And every time they ask,

in that moment before I answer, I think
of my lost possessions, the things

those frigging Mayflower people sent on
to someone else. I growl. I imagine

what a dirt farmer in Maroa
must be doing to my recording

of *The Tender Land*, and of how
my dog-eared copy of Kafka's

The Judgement is probably propping up
the tireless front end of his Ford.

But mostly when they ask me,
are you settled in, I move in my mind

to Rockaway, 25 years ago, and watch
my grandfather in the cane seat

of his ladder-backed chair shuffling
a pinochle deck while Bessie, my grandmother

hunches, like Quasimodo, over the dog's
bowl that says ROXIE. She is breaking

Matzo into the dog's favorite, coffee
with cream, two sugars. They do not see me,

they do not see how real the arthritis is
in Roxie's bones, or that soon

some of the card players will be rising
like the smoke of their cigars,

their bets. The dog's tail is keeping
some ungodly rhythm, saying yes, saying

yes, and grandma goes back
to the kitchen. They do not see

the cane of the chairs giving way,
and a few of my grandfather's toes

going, in a year, to gangrene. They
play cards. Someone brings lunch. My new

neighbors come at me again. Are you
settled in? Are you settled in? And I want

to ask *them*, are *you* settled in? Do you
like the cards in your hand? Is that seat

safe? Will you sail the ship on that frigging
green truck and get my stuff back? Do you hear

the bells of sanctuary, of sanctuary, every time
I give you my answer, my yes, my yes, my

dog-tail yes?

ON MOVING TO ILLINOIS

> A good poet is someone who manages, in a lifetime
> of standing out in thunderstorms, to be struck by
> lightning five or six times; a dozen or two dozen
> times and he is great.
>
> Randall Jarrell, *Reflections On Wallace Stevens*

At this very moment, from Kankakee to Carbondale,
from Mandota to Athensville, the State is teeming

with thunderstorms. Poets, I can see them,
are standing, elbow to elbow, in their own

bright buckets of water, fishing like Franklin
with kites, urging the bolts on. The key

is being there, in the open, skeletal as a dead deer
willing to decompose under the peripeteia,

the wheels of a Mack truck. Shamelessness
always helps, as in the long body of the dachshund,

his boring landscape, that saves him from the name
Chihuahua. Archimedes might have said it best,

dumb-struck in Champaign. "Stand wherever I will,
all I get is wet."

TODAY

No one wants to be mortal,
it just happens. The sun
comes up and one day you're
there to see it. Some kid
named, Tickie, is throwing
a newspaper at your feet,
and it lands on the door-
mat your sister gave you,
the one with the fly-fisher-
man arcing a dry-fly
toward some ungodly trout.
In your pocket a knife
is dulling in its rose-
wood case, and your wife
is calling you from the
kitchen, there's a phone
call, and how do you want
your eggs. Sunny-side up
comes to mind and you pick
up what you think is the
phone and your mother tells
you your father died in his
sleep last night. The paper
drops from your hand, opens
to the weather map, your kids
jump down the stairs. They
giggle at a cartoon on the
TV, ignoring the meteorological
hieroglyphs, the low and high
pressure systems battling it
out on the surface of the page.
Your eggs are ready, the dog
barks, the sun draws its bow
in the pine tree and shoots
light hard through the picture
window.

THE PRACTICE FIELD

Scrimmage and the plovers break their cover
from among the drainage rocks of the practice field

where the Riverdale School young women
in their green tartan skirts and plastic

shin-guards are powdering the hard ball across
the dry autumn field. Zeke, the caretaker,

is leaning against the bleachers, peeling
with his fat thumbs the orange he saved from lunch.

He is thinking thoughts he should not, while the pleats
of the girls' skirts fall neatly in and out

of place revealing their smooth private mechanisms,
the way the wing feathers of a bird flare

and expose the white tender sides of its chest
in the slowest of motion. Yet none of the passengers

in the plane banking toward the afternoon sun
are aware of Elizabeth Warner's fine shot

on goal, or for that matter, of anything but the outlines
of boundaries and roads. Soon the snow

will cover all the lines we have drawn to keep the sides
clear. And Margaret, the goalie, will lose the small

roundness of her belly that has made her ill
for weeks. When the real games come they will

move to the other field and the large black scoreboard
donated by a class no one remembers will tell us

what counts.

KEEPING THE BIRDS ON THE GROUND

I walk up to them. Cardinal, starling,
mourning dove. "It's not right," I say.

"Stay on the ground, don't fly anymore,
it's dangerous. You're giving the children

ideas, dreams." But the birds, they just
coo, they turn their heads, they muscle

their wing-feathers like razor shells, or
they just keep looking at themselves

in my car's side-view mirror, and shit
until it crusts like a Jackson Pollack

down the door. I say, "Don't fly
so much, don't risk it. I hear

a Canada Goose fouled the prop
of a Piper Cub." I say, "Look,

they've already tied your hands
behind your back. What's next?"

PEAS

Some things don't want to be
uncovered. My son, in the morning
especially, doesn't want to be

uncovered. The egg, deep in its shell,
tight as the can of coffee, or
the milk, quiet in cardboard, or the chicken,

almost gone in the ice-box, they don't
want to be uncovered. They give you a hard
look, like you've caught them by

surprise, you've been rude when there
was no thought of being rude.
I remember how black sea bass would run

close to the shore at low
tide. Sometimes I would see them there,
through the water at my knees,

darting like comets after crabs or
smaller fish. They were fast.
I imagine if they bothered to look up,

they'd look like my son,
startled, unnerved, insulted by the fact
they were being watched,

simply observed. Sometimes when I open
a can of peas I think
about the universe, about the depth of

darkness, about whether if
the sky full of stars were turned back
like the top of a can, I'd

be angry, annoyed, or would someone
else, looking in
from the other side, complain.

INNOCENCE

Even as the poem begins
it wants
to end. Knowing
that should you give an old horse full rein
it would head
for the barn. Knowing this, and that
most birds make many nests, you must start
with something like—

> I walk down the hill. I walk back.

Or,

> The Aztec-orange school bus, absolute as the
> amaranth, is making its rounds.

HIDING

That Sam-I-am!
That Sam-I-am!
I do not like
that Sam-I-am!

Green Eggs and Ham
by Dr. Seuss

The lights go off, and since I am ten,
beyond night-lights or my father

reading to me from Dr. Seuss, the non-
kosher, *Green Eggs and Ham*, I watch,

for a moment, the car lights from
the street below our apartment send

images up through the evergreen, through
the cross-hatched casement window, and form

colorless finger-paints on my bedroom
ceiling. Friendly, at first, they move

like birds' wings splaying before flight, or
the pleats of my mother's dress, that so

tightly ironed seem to have been given
the order, ATTENTION, retracting before

they spin away from her as she turns
in her closet mirror. Soon, like some

innocence betrayed, or God in great
delusion, I see on the ceiling Lon

Chaney, Boris Karloff, Vincent Price and
the pendulum cutting like Snidely Whip-

lash, me tied to the log nearing
the buzzsaw. I am under the sheets,

the red plastic flashlight hides
from my frantic right hand that wants,

like a drowning person air, something
to hang onto, a chance to bring into

this tent, this cave, any illumination. When
I feel the flashlight fall from the night-

stand, from that desperate swing of my
arm, from my fingertips, its fall and

bounce on the glossy oak plank that is
barrier, the ceiling of my downstairs

neighbor, Diane Desimone, the girl
I love, my older sister's best friend,

I am ashamed of myself, such noise. But there,
now, when I think of her in my Lascaux, I am

painting, hiding from thoughts, pictures,
that will leave me when sleep comes, when

sleep goes, wet in my bed
by morning.

            The next day, my mother
goes shopping, leaves me, thank God,

downstairs with Diane. She thinks, even
now, that I am forty-one, looking back,

that I cannot see Diane's proud breasts
forming in that starched school shirt. Diane

says, "Hide and seek. I'll count to
twenty." And I, a field-mouse with

a death wish coursing in and out
of the hawk's shadow, will try under

the sink, the sticky roach traps rich
with armor, a closet, a bed, but first,

until she counts to seven I just look
at her, her palms flush to her cheeks,

standing still in the center
of her living room, her mouth

forming the count, "One, Two..." And
when she gets to two syllables, to, "SEV-EN,"

her mouth in slow motion could be saying
anything, could be eating a peach. I run,

I can't stand it anymore and I hide, I
hide in her mother's closet, the soft

skirts and dresses give, even at ten,
desire away. And I want her desperately

not to find me, hard, standing behind
her mother's red, black, open-toed

heels. "Fifteen," I hear her say,
and I think of her mouth. Her

knees between her calf-high socks and green
plaid St. Vincent's School skirt are all

that I can see. Even now,
imagine.

        When I was young, I thought age
would make me safe, but when the mouse hit

the hawk hard in her stomach because
the rabbi, that day when I was twelve,

said, "You should not have Catholic
friends," I hid in the woods across

the street until her mother called mine
and they dragged me out of the bramble,

the knot of vine. And he, when my mother
got to the temple, her arm like a beak

sharpening in his face, was cornered. He,
the great rabbi, backed up, hid behind

his books, behind his tongue, and he said
he never said it, said I misunderstood. He

struck a match for his pipe in his dark
library and pondered my mother's

legs, her breasts that hid, large
and ponderous under her raincoat.

                    But my mother,
no better now, no better than any of us, when I

visit her near Disney World, who after every
dinner, every meal out, looks into her

compact's mirror, the powder puff hiding
the lines, the time she wasted on her Comet,

her 409, her whisk brooms dull in their
teeth. There, in that mirror, after every

meal, she sees her father standing over
her, yelling like a buzzard behind her head

while she plays her scales to the stiff
beat of the metronome, counting

injustices right and left, right and
left. She sees herself, she sees

me watching her play Chopin on our Chickering,
a sparrow, ill-advised, flying through the opened

bedroom window above the goose-down pillows
airing on the ledge of the red brick building,

a sparrow snatched from the air like hope
itself by the teeth of our pure bred

Schnauzer. She is a child, my mother,
she is a child painting a clown's face

white. With her red lipstick, with her mascara,
with her wall over a wall, she is at war

I think. My mother, there is a war
in her, there is a war

in my mother that she is painting
her face for.

My father is patient, and so
am I. So am I. I am so. I grow my hair

long, a pony-tail at forty-one, the tail
of the mouse, of the mouse of the house. The girls

will love it, dive out of the sky for it. And I
must hide in the last place I know, in the landscape

that is my last bed. But still, frightened,
primitive, my right arm reaching for the nightstand,

I want to know when I hear the count
to twenty under those dark green

sheets, will someone come for me, seek me
in my last bed, bed at last? Hawk, mother,

God,
Diane?

PART 2

THE UMLAUT

for Cornelio Casaclang

There is a decided disadvantage in being
Jewish, especially if, for one reason or

another, one wants, as I have wanted, to use
the umlaut. It is not a great want, like my

wanting a gun-metal blue 911 Porsche, or,
for that matter, Uma Thurman to simply

acknowledge my existence, but in my family, for
my mother, the umlaut might just as well be

that two finger mustache, that comma of hair, that
click of boots, those long arms cordoned in salute,

the high step, the swastika itself incarnate. So I took
Spanish, just to avoid it, and though the tilde,

curvaceous, erotic as a landscape at dusk, had some
appeal, I could never get clear of the umlaut,

so direct, so finally odd. And how we love
such things, the dark beaded eyes of one's mother's

stone martin boa draped in their endless head to tail
romp around her neck. The snake's eyes, the bullet

shots in the stop sign on a country road. The abandoned
moons of two letters "i", the stuttered period gone

aloft, or the abbreviated ellipses, seeking as might some
crazed explorer an explanation for gravity. The capsized

colon, the domino of punctuation, the eyes of Rousseau's
cat splitting the palm fronds. Yet still, whatever

I imagine—my mother's long pointed sewing needles
clicking in each carry and drop, she sees the umlaut as

the scar on her friend's abdomen, the ink on the wrist,
the spot-lights, the points of barbed wire, the last

thing the eyes can hold before it all goes dark. Finally,
I cannot argue with my mother. And even though

I cannot see the things she does, I must wear them. How
strange the umlaut. How odd, the longer one looks

at a thing it almost becomes itself.

FRIEDMAN'S LAST STRAW

> Anything that lives in water, but has no fins
> or scales, is to be held detestable.
>
> Leviticus 11:12

So, I go to get the paper, FOUR
DOLLARS for The New York Times,
who's complaining, a dozen bagels,
three bialys, and a bisel whitefish and
coming from behind the green dumpster
of Rod's Delicatessen is a black panther
the size of a German Shepherd that makes
me hit the brakes of my newly leased
white Lincoln Town Car, the first
Ford I ever had. He moves like Jerry
Block, my neighbor, who just had hip
replacement by that famous surgeon
in Boca Raton, a little tender, maybe
old, as he galumps across Military
Trail, as if the world is nothing
but tuna cans, and Rod's leftover
specials. To tell you the truth
I'm sorry for him, a little. How sad
it's got to be to be scrounging meals
near Century Village where Red Buttons
welcomes everyone with open arms, three
eighteen hole golf courses and two separate
Kosher kitchens. But I've got my own
troubles, Esther is waiting, and up north
in New Rochelle, my son, Steven, is getting
divorced from his shikseh wife who Esther
said he shouldn't have married in the first
place and who'll get half the foundation
business I worked my ass off for, not to
mention the two nitro patches I wear under

my long sleeve shirt, because of the melanomas,
aren't working the way they should. I just
keep holding water even though that prince
of a doctor has doubled the lasix and I feel
like some doped-up gelding at Hialeah. How's
retirement, they ask me, and I can't sleep
ever since I read an article about the mosquitoes
and the alligators breeding like tadpoles
on all the damn water-holes. And then, when
all I can think about is teeth and welts, Eva
Silverstein, Esther's best friend, comes over
with a noodle kugle and says she saw a walking
catfish on the ninth green. That's the last straw.
Catfish is one thing, but WALKING is another.
So, I sit every night, on the balcony, with my
Ever-Ready and Mossberg 12 gauge shotgun, it's
a shandeh, a liberal Jew with a gun, on the balcony
flashing the beam of light back and forth over the
thirteenth green, our apartment overlooking,
the best deal we could get, furnished. I'm
like some air-raid warden, except I'm looking
down, waiting for that detestable slimy devil's
fish to crawl my way. I wonder, what is this place
where God can make that evil bottom feeder
walk from pond to pond. It makes me think
if Mengala has sent them up from Brazil, one
of his lovely experiments, the twisted smile
of that skeiny scaleless heretic of a fish. I
tell you, this world is no place to live in
if you don't have enough to get to the top floor.

MID-LIFE, A PROFESSOR DREAMS

for Bridget Mueller

Above her head a fluorescent bulb is sputtering
for light. Her hand extended, it's too early

for questions. Some guy with glasses and a violin
case is trying to get in before I start the roll.

She says, "Sir?" And she knows I hate that. Her
hand, like an Origami swan, the ones you pull

by the tail and its wings flair, its head drops,
insists. The guy is now folded in his seat.

"What, what is it?" "Sir, do you mind," she
asks, "do you mind if I ask a personal question?"

The preening stops. Pencils quit their twirl. They
look at me, for a moment, like I'm smart.

"Sure," I say, "what the hell." She blinks once,
her hand now down below the desk, she asks,

"How old are you?" I hesitate, I don't know
why. I'm thinking, she's looked at me before,

maybe not. It isn't long before the guy with the glasses
leans down to his instrument case, unlatches, and

starts pulling like he's stuck in the middle of a lake
and the mixture is way too lean. The bulb isn't full

yet. I don't know what to say. What does she want
to know? The guy has a chain saw and now he's

standing next to me, blue smoke coughing past his
elbow. She blinks again. At the waist, he runs

the teeth across me and the others flock around
like I'm money from a Brink's truck. One of them

is counting rings and from my beard I hear feathers—
three crows, a few flickers, a Stellar's Jay head for the door.

And her, the one with the hand, she's just as sweet as
sweet can be, cupped to my ear, whispering, "TIMBER!"

THE PIRATE MAP

for Paul Friedman

If X marks the spot
then it's easier
than I thought. Still,

I keep thinking of
that joke, the one
about the fishermen,

call them Jacques
and Harold, who,
out in the middle

of the reservoir
in their rented boat,
are catching fish, hand

over fist, and Jacques
turns to Harold and says,
"Don't you think

we should mark this
spot?" And Harold
replies, "Sure, I'll

put an X right here
on the side of the boat."
And Jacques, looking

at him with that certain
condescension that only
the French can muster, says,

"That's stupid, that's
dumb. What if we don't get
the same boat!" But Harold,

not willing to be undone,
even by the actual
end of a joke, turns to Jacques

and exclaims, "Do you think
these fish are real!" And
Jacques, who frankly

has already gutted
a dozen or so, and smells
a bit like walleye, looks

to Harold with a fine
mixture of confidence
and bewilderment, Claude

Rains in his gauzy suit,
and says, "You mean,
we have a stringer of NOTHING

dangling from the end
of the boat?" Harold nods
like a rabbi dovening, or

one of those dachshunds
next to the Kleenex box
people put on the shelves

in the back of their cars.
"A stringer of NOTHING.
That's good, Jacques. I

like that. That's ripe,"
Harold says, as he rows
the boat toward the shore.

And I think
there must be a way
to send in Errol Flynn

brandishing a sword
from the mast of a Spanish
galleon, to fire some salvos

broadside, or simply,
move the reservoir,
from here, here

where all the X's begin,
and leave them rowing,
rowing, rowing, rowing

in their treasured air.

THE PROFESSOR

1

Walking To School To Teach My Class

Much is made of Jesus
strolling over the Galilee, of Houdini,
rising from the shackled sunken
streamer trunk. Still, over the years,
I have heard explanations, theorists
that blossom like blue asters, annuals,
useless over the rest of time.
"Halibut," one said. "Halibut. Christ
could have trained the fish
to swim below the surface, and then
he could have walked on them,
like doormats, huge, unmistakable,
fluttering their edges like
Chinese fans under the waves." "And
Houdini, no one ever checked his mouth
for a key, and we know double-jointedness
helps in the escape from straight-jackets."
Here, it is merely Summer. I
am teaching Melville to the dead, and
the heat is reaching the unbearable,
loosening my arms from their sockets
as I walk to school over the shimmering
brick walkway laid in a pattern
called herringbone while my mouth,
the glacier, is giving under the perennial
sun.

2

Knowing Too Much

The clouds are indecisive. For a Wednesday,
there are more papers to grade than there are

those wide dried leaves of the huge sycamore
I refuse to police in my yard. My neighbor

is just now putting out his three plastic
buckets of recyclables. What isn't

blown by the wind is considered almost
permanent. I hear my son crying because

it is difficult at three to button one's
own pants. Clearly this is the real

world. Just by pricking my thumb, I can tell
that. Or by the bills, the carrot magnet

that fixes my next doctor's appointment
to the Frigidaire like blood over the door

jamb. The blind man, next door, is pandering
his cane down the street. Obligation

informs me I must start these papers, though,
somewhere else, I am almost sure, INFINITY

is signing its name Queequeg, in The Book
Of The Dead.

Tenure

The Head comes over with a smile. I know
he must have rented it because the last
time he smiled was when he had a paper

published in *The Wichita Quarterly Review
Of Humanity*, a paper entitled, "Dorothy:
The Phallus Of Tornadoes." But his hand,

ungodly, is out, and I've been six years teaching
in the dark because of budget cuts. He says,
"Congratulations, the committee has reviewed

your file, your teaching record, your letters
of purpose, the FBI investigation, that erroneous
allegation of zoophobia, you have TENURE."

I want to say thanks, but somewhere, in that
grasp, in that handshake, I see, the limp
wings of the white albatross learning

to harden, the hammering of a gold coin
to my forehead. I hear the peg leg of the whole
department walking at night on the deck

of the Pequod. And as I cast my eye to his elbow,
the bend of Ahab's arm, I see Gregory Peck,
as he rises, shackled in harpoon lines to Moby

Dick, that scrimshaw smile of the beast,
fixed—like the rest of my life
to his beckoning.

DECLINATION

Sometimes, I need to know
what's real, what's not. I'll

be sitting in my office, the
second floor of the English

Building and I'll hear a bus
stop, air-brakes breaking from

the street noise I've become
used to. I slide my swivel chair

toward the window, come up
next to the throaty radiator no one

in the Physical Plant has been able
to fix. Frankly, it gets so hot

you could bake cookies on my desk.
Then, I'll begin to crane my neck

to look for the bus, to see if I was
hearing right. But then I'll stop. I'll

begin to wonder if it might be one
of those Budweiser trucks coming

to fill the campus bars off Wright
Street with new metal kegs, those

large bullets of beer they load through
the trap doors I step over on my way

to the Home Of Gourmet Chinese
Restaurant two doors down the block.

I won't move for a moment. I'll just
sit there in my swivel chair close to

the radiator I've nicknamed "Bunson,"
and just think about whether it was

the bus or the beer truck I heard. I
want to be right. That is, before I

look out of the window to be sure
what the noise was, I want to know.

It's a game I play. A game I want to
win. After all, there aren't tigers in

Illinois, no wilderness, no surprises, no
adventures other than guessing if the noise

from air-brakes comes from the beer truck
or the bus. Last week, on my way to the

Home Of Gourmet Chinese Restaurant, I got
behind two physics professors who

were stopped from walking down
the sidewalk by the Budweiser beer

truck delivery man rolling kegs down
the conveyor belt through the trap doors.

They stood there, the two professors,
not wanting to walk into the street and

around the Budweiser truck. They began
to discuss friction, leverage, the difference

between true north and magnetic north. Me,
I leaned against the brick wall of the bar

and tried not to laugh. But what do I have
to be so smug about, I thought. I thought

about some explanation I'd seen on public
television about the earth's plates. How

the guy explaining the whole thing was
using chocolate chip cookies to make his

point about the dynamics of earthquakes,
faults, and fissures. I remembered him

saying the continent of America was moving
two inches from Europe every year. I

thought how nice that would be for Ralph
Waldo Emerson if he were still alive. He

showed how when the cookies, the plates,
overlap, that the downward pressure of

gravity would cause them to break. I moved
away from the wall. I wondered, as I watched

these two professors watching beer kegs roll
down the conveyor belt, if oatmeal cookies

could substitute for chocolate chip. I laughed
to myself. I liked the ease with which the delivery

man, "Bill" it said on his shirt, went about his
work. How he seemed so unperturbed by

the professors watching him. How, when he
finished, he took the uncapped Bic pen from

behind his left ear and made some note about
the delivery on a pad he'd taken from the cab.

How the whole thing reminded me of ships
waiting for a draw-bridge to open, or

the cars on the same bridge, or planes passing
over the boats and the cars at some higher, but

no more significant altitude, I wasn't sure. I became
sad, as I do sometimes. Sometimes when I guess

it's the bus and it turns out to be the beer truck, I
get sad, disappointed. Sometimes, I think I've

let the whole world down by being wrong. Sometimes
though, when I look at the satellite dish on the Engineering

Building on Green Street, the angle of elevation, I
remember Jennifer Jones in "The Song Of Bernadette"

looking up at the Virgin Mary—or maybe not. And then,
then I'm sure the whole town doesn't care what I see.

And maybe I should just roll the chair back
to the desk, not worry about being

right—
wrong.

BULL

Language interrupts us. It's the bison,
strolling across the Turnpike at noon,

the articulature of clothing the beggar
has strewn next to the entrance of the
restaurant Jerome is taking his secretary

to. It's Italian, French, Continental, which-
ever you think is more expensive. He will step
over the legs of the poor bastard with his

palms up and ask Maurice, the maitre de,
for his table. "Good afternoon, Mr. Cunard.
Nice to see you too, Ms. Winther." They will

make their way to the corner booth. And after
she slides along the deep seat of vinyl, her
hose having made a deep tug on his lust, Jerome

will tell her, again, what she needs to hear. He
tells her because he senses departure in her voice,
a ship pulling out of the dock, streamers being

thrown, a bucket of ice embracing the thin neck
of a dark green bottle. He will hold her hand
in both of his, because he knows words are not

enough. Perhaps, there will be a bribe, something
that will turn everything into nouns. Going home,
after work, he'll see the damn buffalo, hunch-

backed and lonely. He'll call his wife on the car-
phone, say, "Dear, you'll never believe it, there's
some beast on the Turnpike, I'm going to be

late." For Beverly, the last straw was last
week, but she doesn't know it yet. She says,
"Honey, could you pick up a pizza at Angelo's,

no anchovies and a six-pack of Diet Coke."
Jerome thinks he hears someone in the back-
ground saying, "Extra cheese." But it's five

o'clock, the kids have band practice. "Sweet-
heart, who was that?" "The radio," she says.
But he can see her, her arm waving like some

anxious bird whose other wing is broken. "Okay,"
he says, "I should make it home in an hour."
"Don't rush, Jerry," she says. He hates it

when she calls him Jerry. Soon the thing
ambles to the side of the round. Traffic
starts to uncouple. All the brake-lights

go dumb. We're moving again, and it's all
because of the bull.

RUMOR

Phyllis is sick of Peter. Peter's
wife, Eunice, has just shot their pet
Doberman four times through the heart.

The neighbors could give a shit, except
that their dandelions have wilted
from the smell of gunpowder.

You would think this would be enough
to make me move from the neighborhood.
But why should I? I was here first.

It's not easy to get an apartment
in this town, and I've just painted
a mural of The Battle Of San Juan Felipe

on my bedroom ceiling. Besides,
I don't live by Phyllis or Peter
or Peter's wife, Eunice, or

their dead Doberman. As a matter of fact,
I don't live in the same town, I don't
even know who they are, that's

the nature of rumor, it just spreads
like newlyweds looking for a better
position. For myself, I don't have anything

better to do but listen while I take
my dirty clothes to different cities
each week to get them cleaned. Last week,

some lady in Cleveland, at Wolfie's
Laundromat, a lady who looked a lot
like my ex-wife, said, "You know,

you look a lot like my ex-husband. I
hated him. He did his laundry in different
cities each week." I looked at her, hard,

to be sure. Then, when I was convinced
she was at least three years older than
my ex-wife, who I hadn't seen in three years,

I showed her my boxer shorts signed by a girl
named Phyllis. What could she say? She said,
"John, take your shorts and go back to Hannibal."

I said, "Gladys,
how did you know
my name?

Did you hear what happened to Eunice's dog?"

LETTER TO MY EX-WIFE WHO IS HAVING LUNCH WITH HAROLD BLOOM TOMORROW

Dear Mariana, Our lives are full of accident and I know
that is no way to start a letter, particularly if you choose
to share it, if I may be so bold as to be familiar, with
Harold. This morning, when I saw the red Rufous Hummingbird whine
in its display flight through the rhododendrons that line
the gate to the convent of Discalced Carmelite Nuns near the top
of Greenhill Road, I was of course reminded of our telephone
conversation about "Variations On A Summer Day," specifically the line,
"Damariscotta da da doo." But leave that to another note. The stars,
now, as stars are out West, are larger even than the keen eyes of the weak-
fish that thrived once near the shores of New Haven. I have been
much interested in night, its demarcations, the land's
end poem that comes as seldom to my shore as Kansas'; and
the moon, the green moon that Stevens hardly speaks of
directly, which is large in the circle of things. Not that I care much
to talk of anxieties or almonds but lately, in talking
with you of your troubles, I am as impotent as a Jew without a sense
of judgment. Here, where the trees still remember how to grow
and salmon show themselves whole in the river, not dressed like Diane
Von Furstenburg on a Wedgewood platter at the Yale
Alumni Luncheon, I must admit to some
jealousies. I think I could love Harold,
myself, were it not for bad dreams and all that deconstruction
and angst spread like chopped-liver at a rabbi's funeral. But I did
not start this letter to raise such subjects as Flaubert's
umbrellas, the six D.A.R. women, tight-lipped and stealing
glances at the newly professed Benedictine running
in cut-offs through the rain, or my cousin, Milton
Finkel, whose name is still an embarrassment. I don't know why
I started this, at night, I would tell you if I knew, when I could be walk-
ing under the pale green water
tower that rises, as a matter
of fact and not significance, like
so many other things. Sex

was always a problem for us. I could never concentrate well,
and for that I am sorry. But who's to say
that in its own way life wasn't better
without sweating and puddles on the sheets. If
Harold lays a hand on you
I'll kill him. Love, Ramon.

GRAVITY

for Kim Vollmer

The last thing the world needs is another poem about angels,
but I can't help it. I've never been good at science,
or wanted to be, since Mr. Zukowsky, my 9th grade science

teacher said, "The earth is moving two inches closer to the sun
each year. You're going to die," he said. "We're all going to
burn up, VAPORIZE," he said. "But still," he added, "you all

have time to read one full length novel." Who could argue
with such illumination. So now, I'm the teacher. Creative
writing, of all things. And last week, I'm arguing with a student

about the TRUTH. I tell her, we need to LIE. She says she can't.
I say, "Look, I know you're Catholic, but the Bible is parable."
She says, "I know you're Jewish. I don't LIE." I figure it out—

I'm barking up the wrong tree. I say, "Try to walk across campus
and think of everyone naked. Naked as TRUTH. No clothes." She looks
right at me, up and down. She starts to laugh. I say, "We are all

the fictions we want to be." I say, "There's this kid, Kevin,
in my afternoon class, he wears a blue bandana." I say, "I know
he doesn't have a headache, but he wears it all the time." I say,

"My ex-wife used to spend hours dressing to look like a Bohemian."
My student says, "Okay, enough, give me an assignment. Give me a
word," she says, "to write from." I look right at her, she knows I don't

like to give assignments. I think of the word ENDOWED. I think
higher and I say, "GRAVITY." Her nose twitches. I say, "GRAVITY,"
again and she knows I'm serious. A few days later, she calls me

at home, tells me she can't make this week's appointment. She says
she heard a story about GRAVITY and she hasn't had time to get it
down. I say, "How about Wednesday?" She says she has to go to

Mass—something about the Virgin Mary, a feast day, assumption.
I say, "Where are your priorities?" She says, "Why don't **YOU**
write a poem about GRAVITY!"

                        Mr. Zukowsky hasn't burned up yet,
but I won't call him. I think it must be angels though, invisible,
their small hands holding us down, keeping us from floating away,

wandering from our lessons. Sometimes, I can feel their perfect
fingers loosen, release, letting me go like it's a game they play,
then pull me back. I can almost see the little gargoyles smiling

like Mr. Zukowsky, next to his Periodic Table that he's just pulled
down over the blackboard, his finger loosening from that small
hollow moon that begins swinging back and forth, trying so hard,

by itself, to come to rest.

PART 3

THE PROMISE

for Tejas Mehta

You've seen them dead in the street. Birds—
pigeons, sparrows, hawks fallen from the sky.
You think, at first, they were just tired
of it all, seen everything, enough, couldn't
think their way out, they just dropped dead
in the middle of a flap. But that's not it,
I know, that's not it. I've been told everything
has a promise. Everything. Seeds, people,
clouds. I've been told the acorn already knows
that it is large, that the tree inside it
is waiting to be filled. That nests
are being made in the mind of a crow
that isn't born yet. It is hard for me
to believe too. But I tell you, I believe
it now. I have seen planes fall from the sky,
people stop dead in the street. Just yesterday,
a plane flying from Kanpur to Katmandu crashed
into the side of a mountain, the pilot repeating,
"I see the airport, I see the lights. We're
coming in." You say, "It wasn't there." I say,
he saw it. I say, he saw an airport that wasn't
built yet and birds are flying into promises. I
know it's hard to believe. We all hit something.
I've been told, this is the dark room
we practice being blind in.

REVELATION IN THE LOBBY OF THE GRAND HOTEL

We disclaim the body, as surely

as the ground surrenders the plane to the air
and later retrieves it. I have watched,

in the presence of angels balancing
on silver trays an afternoon of hi-balls

in the lobby of the Grand Hotel, the neat manners
of waiters, the white towels draped like wings

over their forearms mimicking the large wooden blades
of the slow ceiling fans. They slice

the air as delicately as the chef's knife
baring the breast of the ring-necked pheasant,

the meat gathering in his open hand, assuming
a new order. And I have watched the persistent

fountain, whose coins work out odd wishes, cleansing
itself with the water that rises and falls as if to protect

its ministry from the earthy prayers. Watched
the stately model who has spent the day entombed

in the salon and the old couple, carrying costly relics,
pleased to have simply made it, without incident,

through the revolving door. All the entrances and exits:
luggage racks pushed by bell boys; messages left

in key boxes; the tireless decorator fussing
over the placement of the blue cloisonné. Certainly

there is confusion. Still the guests are sure,
through all their travels—Paraguay, Kyoto, Grand

Rapids, Peru—their trunks will find them. As it has come
to me the spirit, no matter where it lands,

is entitled to its things.

THE INCONVENIENCE OF THE SPIRIT

Sometimes it just wants you to take a train ride, a long
walk in the woods, a ride in the country. It wants you

to see deer in the mist, bats circling the pagoda shapes
of fir trees at dusk. It wants you to kick acorns down

some dirt road behind the corn field. It has the nerve
to move you from the corduroy couch in the den

to your feet when all you really want is to sit, be still. It tells
you when someone dies before the phone rings, when the wind

is bringing the big storm. It talks to you when you don't want
to be talked to, in places, in situations, where talking isn't

apropos. It is a loud voice, and such an inconvenience. Sometimes—
and you're not sure if this is the worst,

it will take a trip by itself.

TOURISTS IN THE WRONG CLIMATE

Elegance in the afternoon. They are serving
lunch on the sun-terrace,
where the couples, beneath their neat straw
hats and canopies labeled
Cinzano, cut prosciutto laid over adroit
sections of honeydew.
They are overwhelmed by the orchestration of yellow-
birds swerving, toying,
proprietously peeping under and over the awning
that shades, from the rude
sun, the large fish ice-sculptures at each end
of the long buffet.

In the bay, the dumb, gawky pelican
dives like a drunk pushed
from a tall building in a heavy breeze, comes
up with mullet and
throws his head back over his shoulder sliding
the catch down his gullet.
He wipes his beak on his sleeves as the flesh
bag shakes and sags,
heavier, flapping in the water.

One would like to imagine the proper
little yellow-birds
plastering themselves to the palm trees
in the Hotel's reflecting
glass, or the unmannered pelican inviting
his uninvited appetite
to the huge buffet, where he bags the ice-
sculpture, or that tourist,
who earlier annoyed him, by coming too close,
testing, with his toes, the bay.

UPON DISCOVERING THE MEANS
BY WHICH THE WATERS
MAY FLOW

Exactly. As if you'd known it in another
life. Apples, their various names collecting

unattended under trees. And this much
is given, that the snake invents

the players and they, in turn, make shoes
of his skin. Delivery, we must assume,

rises like a lake to the skirts of darkness,
arranges itself according to the stars, and

coy as a sandpiper, recedes. Snow, if
it is late in coming, seems large, rabbinical

in its heavy fall, collecting questions that half
answer themselves. Why me? Or, why him? This

is evident, light does much to the water
it may pass through.

SPRING IN THE ORANGE GROVE

Winter Park, Florida

In the slight wind
            that courses the lake,
the palm fronds rehearse for Cleopatra,
while the coots, whose white beaks
            betray their dark bodies,

paddle among the lily pads
            watching the bass play
Pharaoh to the fleeing blue-gills. The grove
is full of suns, the paradox of oranges,
            whose hand-blown skins

are tough as the rugged
            back of the dozing alligator
some goldsmith has tooled with an elegant and ancient
geometry. Over the grove the oaks
            and pines stand magnanimous,

dying. They brim with witness,
            the strangled proclamations
of peacocks shattering the dark windows of soldered
moss, the mourning dove's colorless coos,
            and the proud calls

of the redwing parading
            his epaulets among the cattails.
The grove is full of suns, and the mind, Copernican,
coils like a black snake about its peculiar
            egg. It is done, done

with the bright heavy
            oranges falling to the sands,
done with the endless allusions to pyramids,
done with the fanned peacock's innumerable
            eyes, embalmed this season

in beauty.

THAT WING

Mid-June and I think just Giotto
could do justice to that wing. If that wing
were a hand and that hand were the hand of a nun
and he could see the dart of that dark-headed jay's
China-blue feathers slur through the wood. It is not hard to see
that wing as that hand crossing the chest of wood with constancy; I think
just Giotto this June could do justice to a sense that has no body.

IMPERATIVES

for Robert Ardrey

the moon is the white crescent of the blue-winged teal
that sustains the flight of evening in the marsh—

as the bird is man-gibing in a ruffled bath
the morning comes behind

the ladder of light that runs for shore
and dabbles in the mud—

everything is schooled
like the ladyfishes and their kings

dying cautiously from age, old
defending private lithospheres—

as it is all mornings in the Congo forest,
Mackensie basin, Kalahari desert, Andaman and Manhattan islands

we flower with spinal clusters
and fight for day with a yawn

in the thunder of webs
that beat the water for air

ABIDE

for Rashid Robinson

Speak to the angels.
Speak to the angels,
I dare you. Speak
to the angels
as the tulips must,
in their onion skins,
in their dark rooms. Speak
to the angels,
in your thin skin that sheds
as the tulips must, that sheds
as wings must. Speak to the angels,
speak to the angels
in that dark cell
as the tulips must. As the tulips
must remember who they are,
what colors they hold
in their onion skins. Speak
to the angels. Speak
to the angels, as the tulips
must speak to the darkness
around them, must speak
in the cell of themselves
reminding themselves
they are tulips
in a dark cell
speaking to angels. Speak
to the angels. Speak to the angels,
I dare you. Speak
to yourself, to your onion skin
that must shed as the tulips
must, as the tulip must
to climb from the dark
cell. Speak to the clods
of dirt, to the dimes

of stone, to the earthworm
contracting his furrow. Speak
to the angels, I dare you. Remind yourself
as the tulips must remind themselves,
they are tulips, they are tulips
of a certain color, they are
tulips speaking to the angels
of dirt, speaking to themselves
of wings. Speak to the angels,
as the tulips must, as the Winter must
speak to itself of failure, of tulips
reminding themselves they are tulips
of a certain color climbing
from the cell of themselves. Speak
to the angels, I dare you,
as the tulip must
in its onion skin
send the message from its dark cell. Send
its color in a green suit climbing
from its dark cell, where it speaks
to the angels. Speak to your color,
to your dark cell climbing
to the deer rubbing its new helmet of antlers
on the rivers of bark. Speak
to the angels, I dare you,
I dare you to remember
the cell of yourself climbing
through the shed of wings, through
the darkness, through the mouths
of deer, through the helmet of night. I
dare you, speak to the angels, as the tulips
must, as the tulips must, shedding
their mansion of skin.

WHITE DEER

Dog. Unicorn. Deer. I find you on the way
Up my driveway, glaring at my car, as the target

Glares at the arrow. But the car stares back,
Losing its headlights' steel light in the powder

Of your powdered coat. And I think, at first,
You are a neighbor's dog, but then, believe

You leapt the fence of that medieval tapestry
And landed in the cloister of my woods. Dog.

Unicorn. How hard you stare this metal down,
As if it were some awkward armor you outran

A thousand years before. Too soon I see the rest,
Your family in dark suit behind you, standing

Like stone near the salt block, and I conjugate
Again. Dog. Unicorn. Deer. And all

That mystery once allowed succumbs to fact.

DOG

You should know this. You
should know this about
yourself. That in yourself,
the self wants to be
round, to turn, to draw
together as a blue-tick hound
might turn under the moon-
light on a porch on some hill.
Kentucky, maybe. Wrestle
with its ear, give its hind leg
to a small cricketing—then
ponder, not seriously, The Sea
of Tranquillity asserting itself
through the star magnolia, and think,
who cares who named it, what
difference does it make that some dimpled
golf ball may be in orbit there. You
need to know this about yourself. That the cold
certainty of things, the moon, has nothing
to do with your dogness. And the hill
the porch is on, the one on which the dog
is readying for sleep, is not particularly
high, nor particularly low, so when the fog
comes in the morning, it will never
settle fully on your back, it will ride
through you, over you, like an anger, a stream
of albino ants looking for their station—that
is the fog. But you are the dog. And if you have
trouble, trouble beyond itch, it is your sense
of smell. You can smell the hot whippet high
in her heat miles away, the surly wing-feathers
of the goldfinch preening near a fester of dick-thistle.
You can smell that. And you can smell
the cat edging along the school yard fence
looking for the open window. It could keep you
awake. You could snarl, turn rabid, imagine yourself

poised in a mural, a Rufino Tamayo, perhaps. But then,
there's no need to be clever, symbolic, you should
know that, that the self wants the self, no matter
where it wanders. Even if the dog takes to running,
breaks through a creek after something small, fast,
a rabbit praying for boredom. You should know
this. It's all toying—right up to the end,
when the fur is gone from the skin, the day
gone dull into stars. You should know this.
We will all turn dog, nose to tail, nose
to tail, the ear finally rested
by the heart.

The author is grateful to the University of Illinois, The Illinois Arts Council, and The New Jersey Council On The Arts for their generous support. And, to no lesser degree, the author wishes to acknowledge the brutal kindness of his friends in helping to realize this project.

PHOTO: MACKLIN MADONICK

Michael David Madonick is an Associate Professor at the University of Illinois. He was born and raised in New York City and educated at Rollins College and the University of Oregon. He is a recipient of the Academy of American Poets' Prize, the New Jersey Council on the Arts "Distinguished Artist" Award, an Illinois Arts Council Grant, and an Illinois Arts Council Literary Award. His poems have appeared in numerous journals, anthologies, and literary magazines, including BOULEVARD, NEW ENGLAND REVIEW, EPOCH, CHICAGO REVIEW, AMERICAN LITERARY REVIEW, SOUTHERN HUMANITIES REVIEW, and TAR RIVER POETRY. He lives in Urbana, Illinois with his wife, Brigit, and their son, Macklin.